THE NOTEBOOK OF DOOM

WHACK OF THE P-REX

by Troy Cummings

BRANCHES™
SCHOLASTIC INC.

TABLE OF CONTENTS

To Mason. If I had to rank my nephews, you'd definitely be in the top two.

Thank you, Katie Carella and Liz Herzog, for helping me hack away at this until we got to the sweet surprise.

Library of Congress Cataloging-in-Publication Data

Cummings, Troy, author.
Whack of the P-rex / by Troy Cummings.
pages cm. - (The Notebook of Doom ; 5)
Summary: When Alexander and his friends find a very large footprint and piles of candy everywhere, they realize the school is being threatened by a Piñata-saurus Rex, a sweet-tasting monster who likes to smash things–and they find that the solution may be as near as a broken ant farm.
2. Ants–Juvenile fiction. 3. Elementary schools–Juvenile fiction. 4. Friendship–Juvenile fiction. 5. Horror tales. [1. Monsters–Fiction. 2. Ants–Fiction. 3. Schools–Fiction. 4. Friendship–Fiction. 5. Horror stories.] I. Title. II. Series: Cummings, Troy. Notebook of doom ; 5.
PZ7.C91494Wh 2014
813.6--dc23
2013050556

ISBN 978-93-5103-453-7

Book design by Liz Herzog

First Scholastic printing, September 2014

This reprint edition: April 2026

Printed in India

CHAPTER 1

BED BUGGED

Alexander watched the six-legged creature creep out of its tunnel. It wiggled its antennae. Then it lifted a big white crystal above its shiny black shell.

Alexander leaned in. There were a hundred more of these things crawling around.

"Hey, kiddo," said Alexander's dad. "Is that an ant farm?"

"Yeah," said Alexander. "We've been studying ants all week for science class. Our farms are due tomorrow."

"Look at them go!" said Alexander's dad. "All those legs and antennae! And those sharp jaws! They give me the willies!"

Alexander smiled. "They're just ants, Dad!"

"I know, Al," his dad said. "But they are so creepy!"

Alexander had seen things *much* creepier than bugs since moving to Stermont. He had seen monsters! Slimy, drooling, chomping, honest-to-badness monsters! The town was full of them.

"Creepy or not, your ant farm is awesome," his dad said. "I'm super proud of you, Al."

Alexander smiled. "Thanks, Dad!" He gave his dad a good-night squeeze and climbed into bed.

"Sleep tight!" said Alexander's dad. He pointed to the ant farm. "And don't let the bedbugs bite!"

Alexander waited for his dad to close the door. Then he reached under his pillow and pulled out an old notebook. He had found the notebook on his first day in Stermont and had been studying it ever since. It was filled with drawings and notes about monsters.

Alexander started to open the notebook — but then froze. He could hear the faint **SKRITCHH, SKRITCHH** of the ants digging around. Or, at least, he thought he could.

Well, he thought, *maybe ants are a* little *creepy.*

He buried his head under his pillow.

CHAPTER 2 FALLING INTO STEP

"Why are you walking like a zombie?"

Alexander knew that gruff-sounding voice without looking up.

"Good morning, Rip," he said. "I'm trying to keep my ant farm from shaking. I don't want to mess up the tunnels!"

"Yeesh," said Rip. "It's just a box of bugs. Who cares?" He gave his ant farm a toss in the air.

Alexander kept his eyes on his ants.

"Oh, great," said Rip. "Here comes another zombie — and this one's wearing a hoodie!"

Nikki shuffled into view, holding her ant farm at arm's length.

"Go kiss a balloon goon, Rip!" she said.

Alexander laughed. Rip and Nikki were his two best friends, and this was about as good as the two of them ever got along. Together, the three friends were the only members of the Super Secret Monster Patrol — the S.S.M.P. They went to school by day and battled monsters by night. And morning. And late afternoon. Weekends, too.

"You guys can take baby steps to school if you want," said Rip. "But I'm not going to creep around like a sleepwalking zombie because of some weenie ants! That's just — Oooh! Candy!"

Alexander peeked over his ant farm. Pieces of candy lay scattered all over the sidewalk. Rip was on his knees, scooping up as much candy as he could.

"Don't eat that!" said Alexander. "You don't know where —"

"Too late!" said Rip. He popped a lemon sucker in his mouth. "Wow! Super sour!"

"Was there a parade?" said Nikki. "Sometimes people throw candy from parade floats . . . and look! There are strips of paper — like confetti — near the curb."

Alexander thought for a moment.

"I think we would have heard if there had been a parade," he said. "Especially a parade where something crashed into a pole!"

Alexander pointed up to a nearby lamppost.

Rip gave his sucker a slurp. "Yow. It's totally wrecked."

"This lamppost was fine yesterday," Alexander said. He took a step back to look at the damage. "That means — WHOA!"

Alexander stumbled and fell backward. Into a huge hole.

"Salamander!" Nikki yelled. "Are you okay?"

Salamander was Alexander's nickname. His friends called him that when they were joking around, doing homework together, or helping him climb out of a big hole.

"Oh, no!" said Alexander. He held up his ant farm. The glass was cracked and the sand was shaken up.

Alexander slid the ant farm into his backpack. "Sorry, ants," he said. "I didn't even see that hole."

"Uh, Salamander . . ." Rip said. He crunched off the rest of his sucker and pointed to the ground with the stick. "That's no hole. It's a giant footprint!"

CHAPTER 3

SWEPT UP

"That footprint was as big as a kiddie pool!" said Alexander.

He lagged behind Rip and Nikki as they walked up the hill toward school. His nose was buried in the notebook.

"What could have made such a supersized footprint?" asked Rip.

"It *had* to be a monster," Alexander said. He flipped to a page with sticky purple thumbprints along one side. "Listen to this, guys."

TRAMPLE HAMSTER

Cute little critter with ENORMOUS feet!

HABITAT That strip of grass between the sidewalk and the street.

SHOE-IN! Trample hamsters wear a size 340.

DIET Anything flat and round. Pancakes, tortillas, baloney slices.

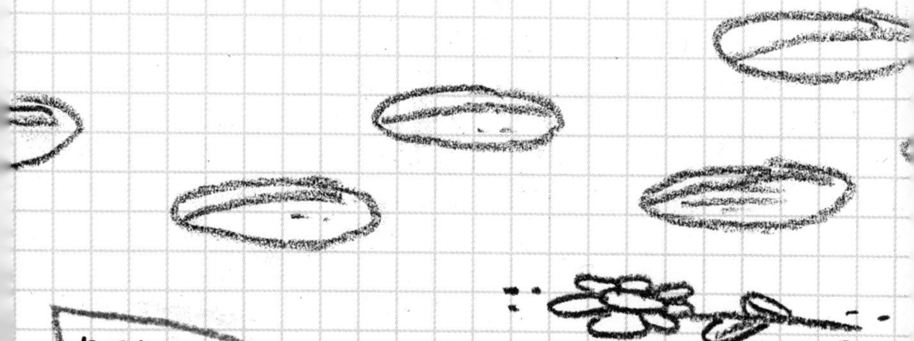

BEHAVIOR Trample hamsters love stomping things flat with their perfectly round, elephant feet.

WARNING! Trample hamsters dislike geese. Waddle around honking to avoid getting flattened.

Alexander closed the notebook. "*Hmm* . . . I'm not sure if our footprint maker was a trample hamster."

"Let's ask the *oldest* member of the S.S.M.P.," said Rip, pointing.

"Him?" said Nikki. "He never wants to help."

They watched a tall, shaky, white-haired man push a tall, shaky, white-haired broom in front of their school.

"Hi, Mr. Hoarsely," said Alexander.

Mr. Hoarsely was the school secretary. He was also the bus driver, the nurse, the gym coach, and today: a janitor.

"Oh, hi," said Mr. Hoarsely. "Ugh! Kids can be so messy! Someone spilled candy on the sidewalk!"

"Candy?" said Alexander. He and Nikki gave each other a look.

"Don't mind if I do!" said Rip. He jumped in front of Mr. Hoarsely's broom to snatch a piece of bubble gum.

"So, Mr. Hoarsely," said Alexander. "We, uh, stumbled across a huge footprint on the way to school. Do you think there could be a trample hamster in town?"

"Well, trample hamsters do have big feet," said Mr. Hoarsely. "They make round footprints, and — HEY! We had a deal! *You* run the S.S.M.P. now! My monster-fighting days are over!"

"But —" said Nikki.

SHISHHH! Just then, the school doors slid open.

"Eep!" Mr. Hoarsely dove into a trash can.

A huge bug-eyed ant monster peeked out of the doors. It had a hard shell, long antennae, and a mean-looking mouth.

The monster's head turned slowly.

"I've been looking for you three!" it said.

CHAPTER 4 SHOWSTOPPER

Actually, it wasn't an ant monster popping out the doors. It was Alexander's teacher, Mr. Plunkett. He was wearing a full-body ant suit.

"Happy Ant Day, students!" he said. "Head to the auditorium right away. We're having a surprise assembly!" He handed Alexander a red flyer.

Grab a seat and guard your sweets for
ANT DAY!
WHERE?
The auditorium
WHEN?
Right now!

"Oh — and, Alexander," said Mr. Plunkett, chuckling, "did something follow you out of the bathroom this morning?"

"Huh?" said Alexander.

"You've got toilet paper stuck to your shoe," said Nikki.

Alexander looked down. Sure enough, a white strip of paper trailed behind his heel. He tore it off and tossed it in the trash.

"Okay, sticky foot," said Rip. "Let's head to the auditorium and get this over with."

Alexander followed his friends into Stermont Elementary, which used to be Stermont Hospital. "This building has an auditorium?" he asked.

They came to a set of doors.

"Yeah," said Nikki. "This used to be the room where doctors could watch other doctors do surgery."

"Ugh. We're going to need surgery on our *brains* after sitting through Plunkett's Ant Day assembly," said Rip.

The three friends sat in the back of the crowded auditorium. A moment later, the lights went out. Rip tossed a piece of bubble gum into his mouth.

Mr. Plunkett came onto the stage in his ant suit. He was wheeling out something tall and flat, covered by a sheet.

"Good morning, Stermont Elementary!" Mr. Plunkett said. "Every year, I have my students keep ant farms. And every year, I collect those ant farms. But where do I put all the ants?"

The crowd was silent. Rip snapped his gum.

Mr. Plunkett smiled. "I add them to THIS!"

He yanked away the sheet, revealing a glass rectangle the size of a billboard. The glass was filled with sand. The sand was filled with tunnels. And the tunnels were filled with ants. Millions of them.

"A giant ant farm?!" said Alexander.

"That's no farm," said Nikki. "That's an ant *city*!"

The crowd cheered. Until a voice shouted from offstage: "STOP!"

Everyone gasped as Principal Vanderpants charged onto the stage. Mr. Plunkett took a few steps back.

"How *dare* you bring these insects into Stermont Elementary!" said Ms. Vanderpants. "Especially after what happened to our *old* school!"

Alexander looked over to his friends. Nikki shrugged. Rip was busy blowing a bubble.

"I, um, er —" Mr. Plunkett said.

"You said that this assembly would be educational," Ms. Vanderpants said. "But instead you've brought in millions of pests! Move this project outside, behind the school!"

She faced the audience. "Students, you'll have lunch early today — bring your backpacks. Afterward, you will have science class outside, on the playground."

The students cheered, louder than before. Mr. Plunkett's antennae drooped as he dragged his ant farm offstage.

"Now," Ms. Vanderpants continued, "I will be giving you a surprise spelling quiz."

The cheering stopped.

"Your first word is —" She paused.

Then she pointed to the back row. "Ripley Bonkowski," she growled. "No gum in school!"

POP!

CHAPTER 5 SHAKE ON IT

After the world's longest spelling quiz, the students headed to the cafeteria.

"Aw, rats," said Nikki. "I miss having pie for lunch."

Alexander, Rip, and Nikki sat at their usual table.

Alexander pulled his lunchbox out of his backpack. It was covered in sand from his cracked ant farm. "Hey, Nikki," he said, "I packed some strawberry gummies for you."

"Thanks, Salamander." Nikki smiled, flashing her sharp-looking fangs. She was secretly a monster — a good monster — called a jampire. Jampires loved red, juicy treats.

Alexander brushed off his lunchbox and flipped it open. **AAAAAGH!** He jumped out of his chair.

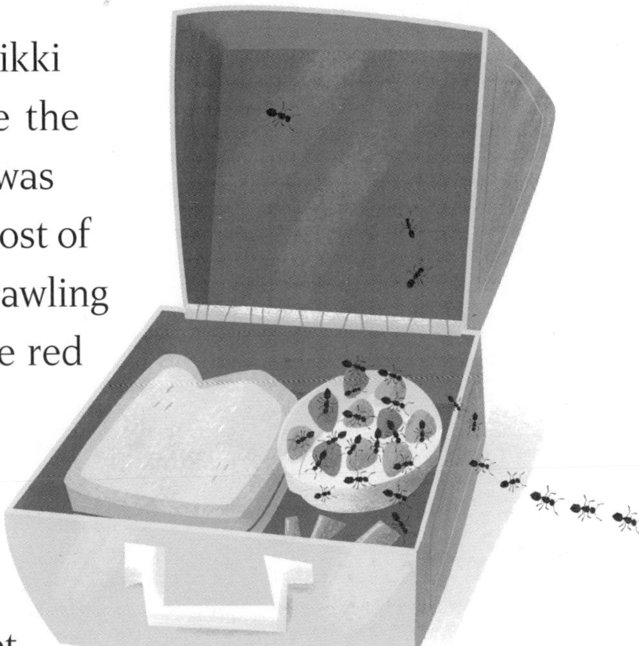

Rip and Nikki peeked inside the lunchbox. It was full of ants. Most of them were crawling around on the red gummies.

"Looks like ants really *do* love the sweet stuff," Rip said.

"Were those ants in your backpack?" asked Nikki, taking an ant-free gummy.

“They must have crawled out of my cracked ant farm,” Alexander said. “So much for *that* science project.”

Alexander sat back down. He checked his sandwich for bugs. There were none. He took a bite as he watched the ants march out of his lunchbox.

“Cheer up!” said Rip. “It’s not like Plunkett needs any more ants! There were a zillion in his giant ant farm!” He tossed Alexander a peppermint.

Alexander made a yuck-face. “Is this more sidewalk candy?”

"Yep!" said Rip. "I still have a few pieces left!"

"Uh, no thanks," Alexander said. He scooted the peppermint back to Rip. "We really need to figure out what kind of monster left that footprint! I don't think it's a trample hamster since the footprint wasn't round. But it still must be big enough to —"

There was a thundering rumble as the whole building shook for a few seconds. The cafeteria grew quiet.

"What was that?" asked Rip.

"Was that an earthquake?!" asked Nikki.

Alexander shook his head. "It —"

He was interrupted by the loudspeaker.

ATTENTION!

This is Principal Vanderpants. You may have noticed a minor vibration. This shaking was likely caused by bulldozers at our new school building down the street. There is no reason to panic.

Alexander watched the ants scurry down the table leg and out of sight. "I think those guys have the right idea," he said.

CHAPTER

6 CRACKED UP

"Class outside is going to be awesome!" said Rip.

Alexander slid his sandy lunchbox into his backpack. "As long as we don't get squashed by the huge-footprint-leaving monster," he said.

Alexander, Rip, and Nikki followed their classmates to the playground.

Rip stopped walking and started laughing.

"What?" asked Alexander.

"Second time today!" he said. Rip pointed to Alexander's left foot.

Alexander looked down. A pink square of paper clung to his shoe. He rolled his eyes and tore it off.

"Line up, everyone!" Mr. Plunkett shouted. He had set up his ant city near the jungle gym. "Have your ant farms out! It's time to move your ants into their new home!"

Alexander watched as the other students gave Mr. Plunkett their farms, filled with ants.

Finally, it was his turn.

"Let's see what you've got!" Mr. Plunkett said.

Alexander handed over his cracked ant farm. Sand spilled to the ground. A single, dizzy ant ran along the frame.

"Uh, sorry," said Alexander. "It kind of broke."

"Well," said Mr. Plunkett, "one ant is better than none." He added Alexander's ant to his ant city. "Welcome to Antville, little guy!" he said.

Then he turned to the class. "Alexander's ant farm may have cracked," he said. "But that won't happen to Antville!" **TOCK TOCK TOCK!** He tapped the thick glass. "A *wrecking ball* couldn't crack this baby!"

Mr. Plunkett nodded toward the school. "I wish I could say the same for *this* place!"

Alexander looked up and gasped.

An enormous crack ran down the side of Stermont Elementary. At the bottom of the crack, there were two wide holes.

"More giant footprints!" whispered Alexander.

"And check it out!" said Rip, pointing. "Another pile of candy."

"The earthquake at lunch —" said Nikki.

"Come on, Nikki, we know it wasn't an earthquake," said Alexander. "It was the huge-footprint-making monster attacking our school!"

CHAPTER 7 HOLE IN THE WALL

Alexander kept looking over his shoulder on the walk home.

"Keep your eyes peeled," he said. "The monster could still be nearby!"

"So, what kind of monster is it?" Rip asked. "It must be enormous!"

Alexander shook some sand out of the notebook. "Here's a super-big one," he said. He read the page aloud.

SKYSCRAPER-SCRAPER

50-story-tall snail, covered in spikes.

HABITAT

49-story-tall buildings.

DIET

Bricks, glass, and steel.

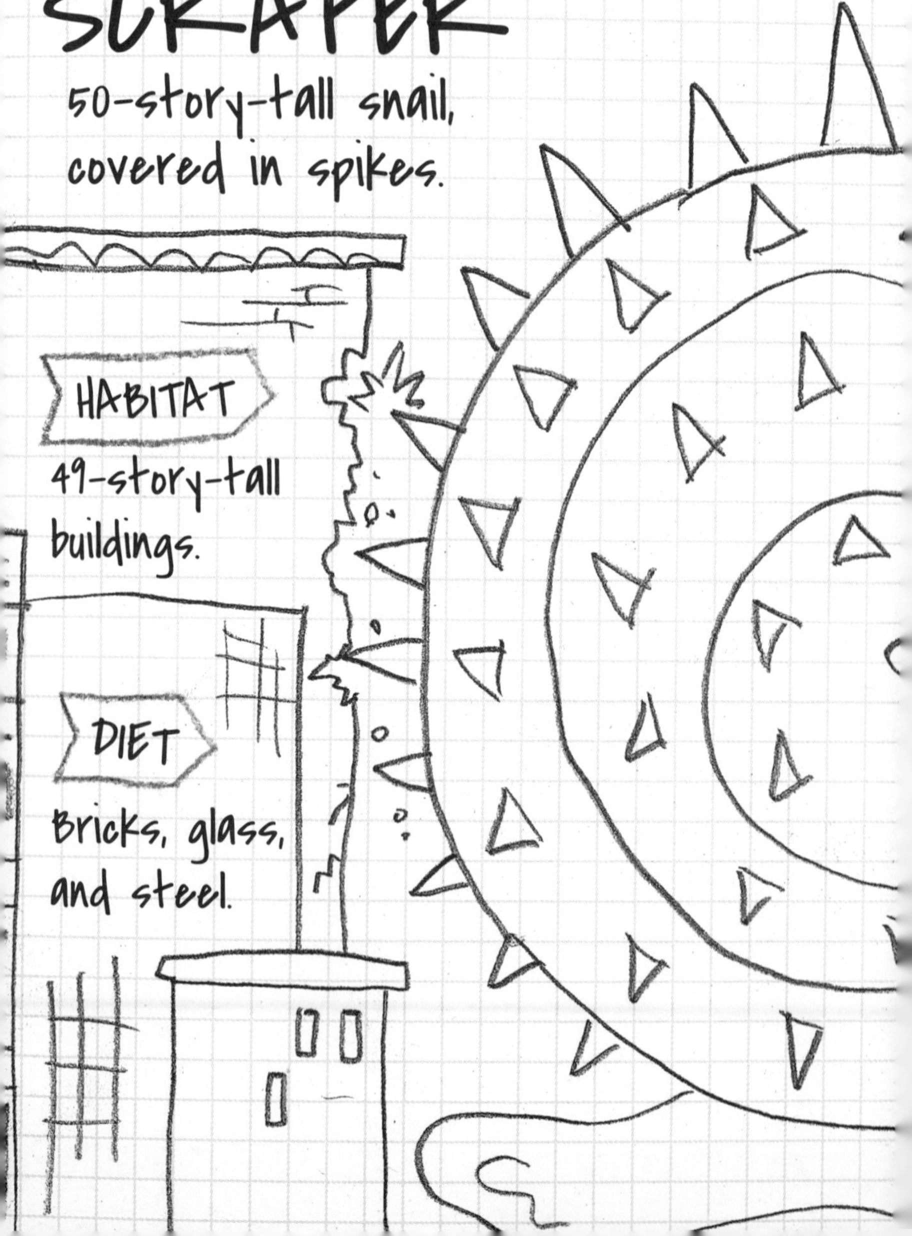

SLOWPOKE! Skyscraper-scrapers always come in last place.

BEHAVIOR This monster grinds its spiky shell against tall buildings. It eats whatever falls off.

WARNING!

Skyscraper-scrapers are only afraid of one thing: French chefs. Carry a spatula and say "BONJOUR" a lot to stay safe.

"What do you think, guys?" Alexander asked, shutting the notebook.

"I don't know," said Rip. He popped a chocolate drop into his mouth. "That snail-thing attacks skyscrapers, not lampposts and grade schools."

"Good point," said Alexander. "I wonder if —"

BBOOOOMMMM!!!

The ground shook. A trash can fell over. Its lid rolled down the sidewalk, stopping at Alexander's feet.

"Did you feel that?" Alexander asked.

The air was still. In the distance, a woman was jogging with her dog.

"Over there! Behind the roller rink!" said Nikki. She pointed to a roundish building nearby.

They watched birds scatter from behind the roller rink. The trees were shaking.

Rip swallowed. "That must be —"

BBOOOOMMMM!!!

The trees shook even more. And then —

GRRAAARRR!

A terrible, lizard-shaped monster rose above the roller rink. It was partly hidden by trees.

Alexander squinted. "Is that a *DINOSAUR?*" he asked.

"I think so!" said Rip.

Just then, the jogger bounced past, talking to her little dog. "Some strange weather we're having! Huh, Sniffy?"

She jogged off, smiling.

"The dinosaur-thing is *right there*," said Nikki. "How could she not have seen it?!"

"Hold on — it's moving!" said Rip.

The monster dropped down behind the big roller rink.

Alexander started running toward the rink. "Come on, guys! We need to get a closer look!"

They ran over and peeked around the edge of the building.

"Where'd that dino-thing go?" asked Nikki, looking around.

"I don't know," said Rip. "But look what it did!"

A huge hole had been smashed into the back wall of the roller rink. There were gigantic footprints everywhere. Hundreds of candies lay scattered about.

"That dino-thing is definitely our building basher," said Alexander.

"But what's with the candy?" asked Nikki. "We've seen gobs of it next to *everything* this monster has smashed."

"Maybe it's bait," said Alexander. "Maybe the monster throws candy around to trap the kids who eat it."

"In that case," said Rip, "let's scram!" He pocketed a jawbreaker.

"Yeah. And I should get home. It's almost dinnertime," said Alexander. "But tomorrow's Saturday. Let's meet at S.S.M.P. headquarters, first thing in the morning!"

"To make battle plans!" said Rip.

"Yes! And in the meantime," said Nikki, "try not to get stepped on!"

Alexander looked back at the extra-extra-extra-large footprints. Then he ran home.

CHAPTER 8 STICKY SITUATION

"Al! You're home!" said Alexander's dad. He was on the front porch, reading the latest issue of Captain Cuspid. "How did everything go with your ant farm?"

"Ant farm?" Alexander asked, looking over his shoulder. "Oh! I forgot about that."

"Really?!" said his dad. "What could make you forget something so important! I bet your ant farm was a big smash!"

"Uh, yeah," said Alexander, "you could say that." His eyes darted to the swaying treetops across the street.

Alexander gulped. "Dad, uh, can we go inside now?"

"Sure thing, Al!" his dad said. "Just as soon as you get that paper off your shoe."

Alexander blinked.

"Not again!" he said. He pulled the strip of paper from the bottom of his shoe. This time, the paper was bright green, and covered in sticky purple goo. *This isn't toilet paper*, he thought.

He touched the goo and gave it a sniff: sour grape. *Taffy?* he thought. *More candy! This must be connected to the dino-monster . . . but how?*

Alexander looked at his sticky, purple finger. He gasped. *Purple thumbprints!*

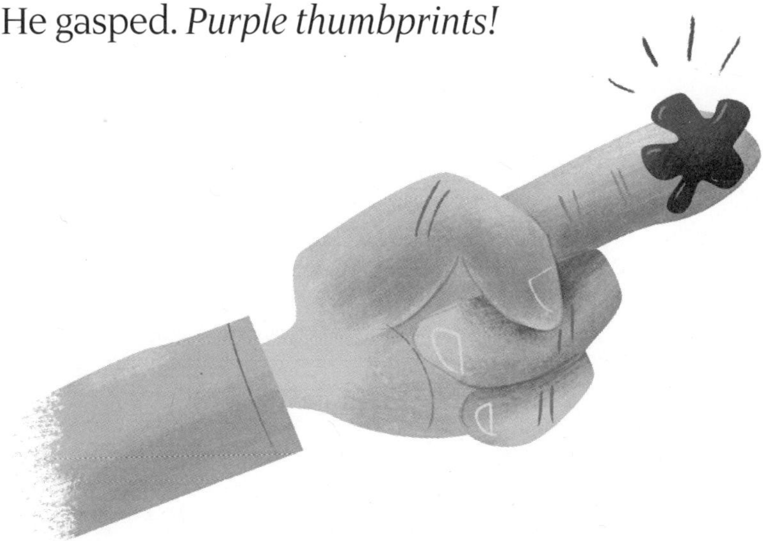

He dashed upstairs to his room. He opened the notebook to the trample hamster pages. Purple thumbprints ran along one side. He sniffed. The page smelled grapey. The next two pages were stuck together by purple taffy! He carefully peeled the sticky pages apart.

"Aha!" he shouted.

P-REX

(Piñata-sa

The P stands for "piñata," like the colorful paper container you bust open at your cousin's birthday party. Except this piñata is the size of a T-rex.

HOWDY! P-rexes are friendly to smaller piñata monsters.

Outdoors. They're way too big to come inside.

They don't eat
thing. That's because
y're full of candy!

P-rexes love smashing
s. The bigger, the smashier!

WARNING! Whack a P-rex before it whacks you! Here's how:

1. Wear a blindfold and spin around three times.
2. Wallop the P-rex with a stick.
3. Watch it break open!

(PSSST! SWEET SURPRISE INSIDE!)

Alexander closed the notebook. Everything made sense now: the giant footprints, the piles of candy, the smashed buildings — even the paper stuck to his shoe.

He couldn't wait to tell Rip and Nikki!

CHAPTER 9 BATTLE PLANS

Alexander raced through the woods bright and early the next morning. He came to an old caboose: the S.S.M.P. headquarters. He rushed inside.

Nikki was studying a map of Stermont. Rip was eating a peanut butter cup.

"Gross, Rip!" said Alexander. "Did you find that on the ground, too?"

Rip nodded. "Yup. Next to a flattened mailbox."

"I wouldn't eat it if I were you. That candy came from our latest monster!" warned Alexander.

Rip swallowed. "Say what?"

Alexander whipped out the notebook. "Look! I found the monster last night. It's right here!" he said. "It's a piñata monster!" He showed the P-rex pages to Rip and Nikki.

"A piñata?" asked Nikki. "Like the kind you break open at birthday parties?"

"Yeah," said Alexander. "And *this* one wants to break things open all over Stermont."

Rip poked the P-rex drawing, leaving a chocolate smudge on its belly. "It sounds like this monster will be easy to beat: We tap it with a stick, and — **POW!** — sweet-surprise time! We'll have a lifetime supply of candy!"

"But the P-rex is enormous!" said Nikki. "How can we hit it without getting smashed?"

"The notebook says the P-rex is nice to little piñata monsters," said Rip. "Too bad we don't know any." He snorted.

Alexander clapped Rip on the back. "That's it!" he said. "We can fool the P-rex! We'll become a little piñata monster!"

"Huh?" asked Rip.

"Here, I'll show you," said Alexander. He flipped over the map of Stermont and started sketching on the back.

"Great plan, Salamander!" said Nikki. She pulled out a box of art supplies. "It's burro-building time!"

CHAPTER 10 FOLLOW THE LEADER

The rainbow-colored paper Battle Burro wobbled to its feet. Seconds later, the three voices inside began to argue.

"You really think this costume will fool the P-rex?" asked Nikki.

"Yes, definitely!" said Alexander. "Probably! Well . . . we'll see."

“You mean *you’ll* see!” said Rip. “*We’re* totally blind back here!”

“If it makes you feel better,” said Alexander, “I can barely see through these noseholes.”

“That does *not* make us feel better,” said Nikki.

The Battle Burro tromped through the woods. It was awkward at first, but after a few stumbles, Alexander, Rip, and Nikki began marching as one six-legged donkey.

"Are we there yet?" asked Rip.

"Not far now," said Alexander. "We're almost out of the woods. . . . Here comes the sidewalk. . . . Okay, turn left NOW!"

The Battle Burro made a wide left turn, and somehow didn't fall over.

"So, if the notebook is right," said Nikki, "we just walk up to the P-rex, spin around three times, and whack it?"

"Exactly," said Alexander. "Oops — birdbath ahead! Swing right!"

"But how will we find the P-rex?" asked Rip.

Alexander put on the brakes, causing Rip and Nikki to bonk heads.

"Uh, that should be easy," he said.

Through the Battle Burro's two noseholes, Alexander could see a path of smashed trees, broken fences, and tilted lampposts. The path was stamped with P-rex tracks that led straight to Stermont Elementary.

CHAPTER 11

DON'T LOSE YOUR HEAD

"GRRRAAAAARR!"

"That sounds loud — and close," Nikki whispered from the belly of the Battle Burro.

Alexander squinted through the costume's peepholes.

"We're here," he said.

They stood in the school parking lot. It was empty, except for one school bus. Behind the bus, Alexander could see the long crack running down Stermont Elementary. He turned his shoulders, craning the Burro's neck around. He could see a mound of shaggy, colorful stuff.

"What do you see?" asked Rip.

"It looks like . . . a big leaf pile," said Alexander. He gasped. It wasn't a pile of leaves. It was the monster's foot.

"Guys," he whispered. "We found the P-rex."

Alexander tilted the Burro's head back to get a better look. The P-rex was covered in colorful strips of paper. It also had tiny arms, a long tail, and teeth the size of tombstones.

BOOM. BOOM.

The P-rex took two giant steps away. Alexander felt the ground shake with each step.

"I don't think it saw us," whispered Alexander.

"What's it doing?" asked Rip.

"I think it's . . . playing," said Alexander.

The P-rex picked up the empty school bus and pushed it around like a toy.

"*Hmm* . . ." said Alexander. "Let's make our move now, while it's distracted." He lowered the Battle Burro's neck into charge position. "Ready?"

The Burro's head bobbled as it tiptoed toward the P-rex.

"Attack now?" asked Nikki.

"Not yet," said Alexander. "We need to get a little closer."

CRUNCH! Alexander stepped on a crackly candy bar.

The P-rex looked up, growling. It squeezed the bus in its claw. The stop sign popped out.

"Guys!" Alexander shouted. "It sees us!"

The friends froze.

STOP

The P-rex tossed the bus aside and stomped over to the Battle Burro. It leaned down, sniffing the Burro's head.

The monster's snout blocked Alexander's peepholes. The inside of the costume went dark.

Alexander tugged a string in the Battle Burro's jaw. The Battle Burro smiled.

The P-rex smiled back.

"Looks like our plan worked," Alexander whispered. "The P-rex thinks we're a little piñata monster!"

"Yes!" Nikki whispered.

"HA!" Rip shouted. "WHAT A DUMMY!"

The P-rex stopped smiling.

"Rip," said Alexander, "I think it heard —"

GLOMP!

The P-rex clamped its jaws around the Battle Burro. And ripped its head off.

CHAPTER

12 BLIND SIDE

The P-rex looked confused by the strange creature at its feet. It had the body of a colorful piñata, and the head of an Alexander Bopp.

"Uh, howdy," said Alexander. He gave a little wave.

The monster roared, firing pieces of candy from its mouth.

Alexander's cheeks stung as he got hit with flying jellybeans. The P-rex raised its huge foot above what was left of the Battle Burro, ready to stomp.

"ATTACK!" Alexander shouted to his friends.

Alexander, Rip, and Nikki tore out of the costume.

They rolled to the side, just as the P-rex's foot came crashing down.

"BLINDFOLDS ON!" Alexander shouted.

Rip and Nikki pulled the bandanas down over their eyes. They each spun around three times. Then they ran in different directions, swinging their sticks like battle-axes.

Alexander circled the P-rex, shouting orders to his blindfolded friends.

"Rip, swing left! I mean, right! Nikki — duck!"

The P-rex didn't know whom to chase. It spun around, nearly swiping Nikki with its heavy tail.

WHIFF! Rip took a swing and missed.

"Guys!" Alexander yelled. "Just come — oof!"

The P-rex snatched up Alexander.

"Salamander?!" called Rip.

"GAHHH!" Alexander cried out as the P-rex squeezed him in its claws.

The monster lifted him up to its open mouth. The P-rex's breath smelled like the inside of a trick-or-treat bag: mint and peanut butter and sour grape and chocolate.

Rip yanked off his blindfold. He ran over to the P-rex and began punching its pinkie toe.

PLOFF!

Alexander kicked the monster in the snout. Colorful bits of paper flaked off its nose.

The P-rex looked back at him, frowning.

Alexander shouted down to Rip. "This big loud monster really *is* just made of paper! We can shred it! Go get Nikki!"

Rip found Nikki. She was still blindfolded, attacking a trash can. He led her back to the P-rex. The monster leaned down, about to grab Rip.

"Hit it, Nikki! NOW!" Alexander shouted.

Nikki gritted her fangs and swung her rake handle hard.

WHACK! The end of her stick connected with the P-rex's belly. Then Alexander went flying through the air.

CHAPTER 13

KER-PLOOIE!

Alexander rolled to the ground. He was shaken but not hurt. A billion bits of paper rained down from the sky.

Nikki tore off her blindfold. "Where's the P-rex?" she asked. "I can't see through all this paper!"

"This paper *is* the P-rex!" said Alexander. "You busted it!"

"Salamander," said Rip, "let's invite a P-rex to your birthday party next Leap Year! We can —"

Suddenly, Rip froze.

"Wait! Where's all the candy?" he asked. "The notebook said we'd have a *sweet* surprise!"

The falling confetti was starting to thin out.

"Uh, Rip," said Nikki. "I found the candy."

"Oh, good!" said Rip, standing up. "Where?"

A monstrous skeleton — made entirely of candy — was standing where the P-rex had been. It had sharp candy cane claws, glowing fireball eyes, and jagged peanut-brittle teeth.

"The P-rex's skeleton!?!" yelled Alexander.

Rip's eyes doubled in size. "It looks like a . . . candy-saurus!"

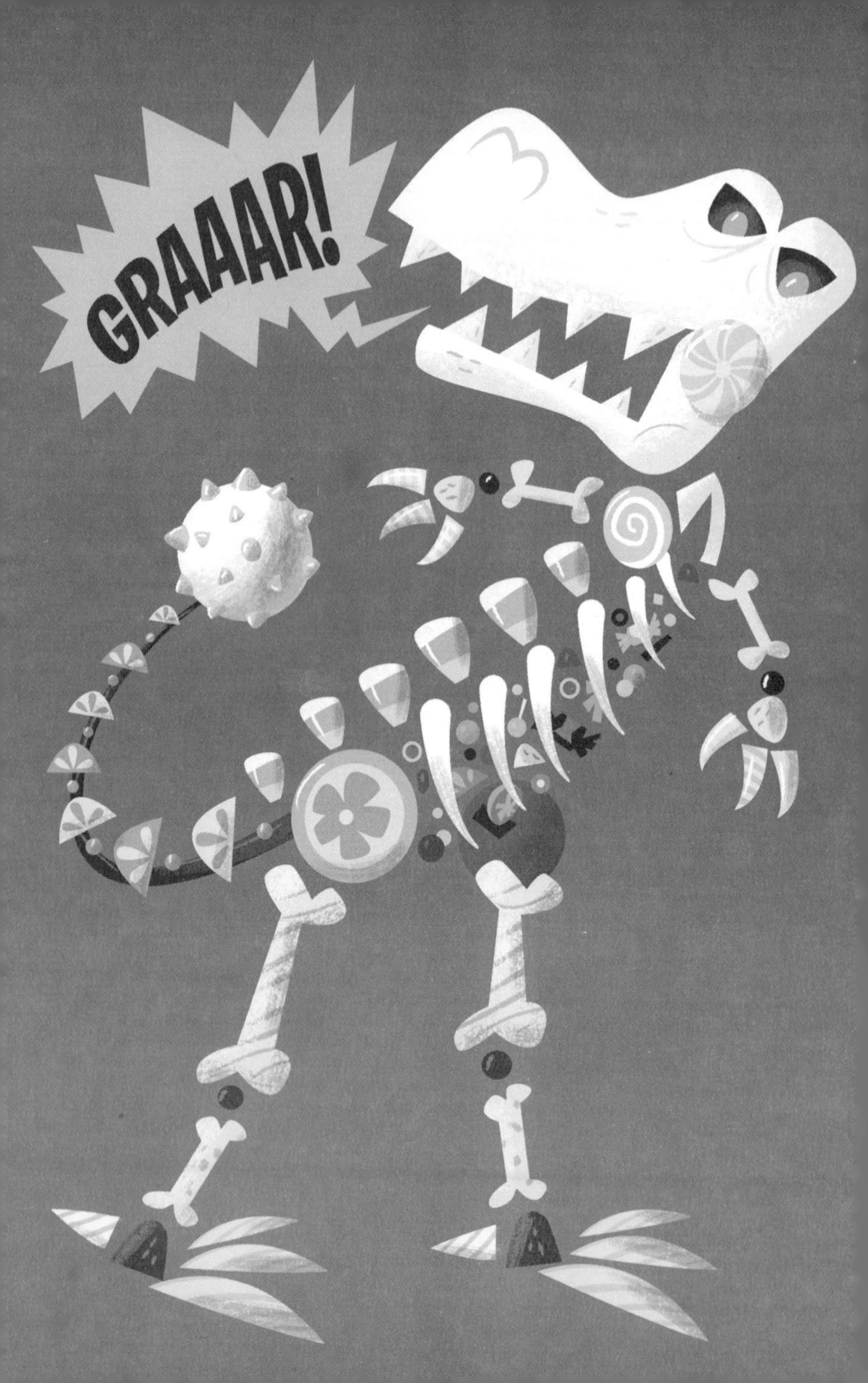
GRAAAR!

The candy-saurus whipped its licorice tail at Nikki. At the end of the tail was a jawbreaker the size of a boulder. Nikki leaped away, just as the jawbreaker crushed the upside-down school bus.

"Run! Its tail is stuck in the bus!" said Rip.

Alexander, Rip, and Nikki darted across the parking lot. The pavement was blanketed with shredded paper and chunks of candy.

They crouched down behind a bike rack.

"Yikes," said Alexander. "This is the biggest monster we've ever —"

SPLONK!

He was interrupted by the sound of a falling school bus.

CHAPTER 14 PLAYTIME!

Alexander peeked over the bike rack. The school bus had been smashed into the ground.

But the monster was nowhere to be seen.

"Where did it go?" asked Rip.

"The monster took one look at you and ran!" said Nikki.

"I'm sure that enormous candy-saurus wants to smash *bigger* things than us," said Alexander. "Things like —"

KARRRROOOOOMM!!!

The ground shook hard enough to rattle Alexander's bones.

"The candy-saurus must be behind the building!" yelled Nikki.

KARRRROOOOOMM!!!

The crack in Stermont Elementary grew a little larger.

"Come on!" said Alexander. "We can't let this monster flatten our school!" They rushed around to the back of the building.

The candy-saurus was near the playground. It bared its teeth as it pounded the school with its jawbreaker tail.

"Look at those claws! And that smashy tail!" said Nikki.

"It is scary looking," said Rip. "But it's kind of slow."

Alexander turned to his friends. "We can bring this thing down. Follow my lead!"

He sprinted across the playground and raced up the slide.

"Hey, fossil face!" he shouted. "Quit smashing our school!"

GRAAAAARRRRR!!!

The candy-saurus stomped toward the slide. It lunged at Alexander. **SNAP!**

Alexander dodged its bite. He zipped down the slide, kicking the monster in the knee.

CRONK! A hunk of hard candy flew off its kneecap.

The monster took a step back.

Rip pumped his fist. "Take that, toffee brain!" he yelled.

Then Rip jumped down onto the seesaw. The opposite end flew up and — **POW!** — socked the monster in the jaw.

The candy-saurus's fireball eyes rolled in their sockets. But the monster picked Rip up and pinned him against the tetherball pole.

It smacked the tetherball with its tail. **WHAP!** The ball twirled on its cord, binding Rip in place.

"Leave him alone!" yelled Nikki. She sailed high on the swing set, kicking the candy-saurus right in its peanut-brittle teeth.

GOOORRRRAARRR-RAAARRR!!!!

The monster turned to Nikki, took a deep breath, and — **BLAAAPPP!!** — shot a stream of purple taffy from its nose.

Nikki tried to run, but the goo hardened around her legs, fixing her to the four square court.

Alexander looked to Nikki, then to Rip. Both of his friends were trapped.

The candy-saurus leaped onto the merry-go-round. It slowly spun around, keeping its glowing red eyes locked on Alexander.

CHAPTER 15

STOMP, CHOMP, AND ROLL

"Careful, Salamander!" cried Rip, tied to the tetherball pole.

"Keep away from its tail!" shouted Nikki, glued to the blacktop.

"Okay!" said Alexander. He zigzagged through the playground. The candy-saurus snapped at his heels, smashing through the playground equipment.

Alexander wriggled into the jungle gym. The candy-saurus reached in with its sharp claws.

"Oh, no! Salamander's trapped!" said Nikki.

"I can't watch this!" said Rip. "Where's my blindfold when I need it?!"

Alexander looked around from inside the metal dome. Everything on the playground was wrecked. Except for Antville.

Candy-cane claws grabbed at Alexander through the bars. Then the monster stuck out its red gummy tongue.

He has a red gummy tongue . . . thought Alexander. *Just like the gummies I brought for lunch!* Alexander looked at Mr. Plunkett's giant ant farm. *Ants love the sweet stuff. . . .*

"I've got an idea!" he called to Rip and Nikki.

"Watch out!" cried Nikki.

GRARRRRR!

The candy-saurus raised its foot above the jungle gym.

Alexander scrambled out from between the bars just as — **CLANK!** — the monster flattened the jungle gym.

Alexander sprinted between the candy-saurus's legs. He skidded to a halt near Antville.

"Run, Salamander!" shouted Nikki.

Alexander planted his feet.

"What are you doing?!" yelled Rip. "Keep moving!"

Alexander looked into the monster's fiery red eyes. "Take your best shot, monster."

GRAH-HA-HAAAR!

The candy-saurus's roar sounded like a laugh. Then it swung its wrecking-ball tail at Alexander.

WHOOSH!

Alexander ducked. He could feel the rush of wind as the jawbreaker shot over his head.

WHACK! The monster's heavy tail slammed into Antville. The giant ant farm exploded. The playground was covered with sand and wood. And, of course, ants.

CHAPTER 16

FEELING ANTSY

A gazillion ants streamed out of Mr. Plunkett's broken ant farm.

"GRAAAR?"

The candy-saurus picked up one foot. Then the other. Soon it was doing a little dance.

Within seconds, the candy monster was up to its gumdrops in ants.

The candy-saurus roared one last time before it was completely covered with hungry ants.

Alexander untied Rip from the tetherball pole.

Thousands of ants chomped away at the taffy that was holding Nikki down. She ran over to Alexander and Rip.

"Guys, look!" Alexander said.

The candy-saurus was gone. The ants had eaten the entire monster, from snout to tail. All that was left was a single sourball.

"I wonder why the ants didn't eat that," said Nikki.

Rip picked it up, brushed it off, and — **GLOMP!** — popped the sourball into his mouth.

Alexander and Nikki stared at him.

"What?" said Rip. "Candy is candy!"

Alexander and Nikki looked at Rip again.

He swallowed. "*What?!*" he said. "So it came from a monster! No big deal."

"I guess we'll find out," said Alexander. He took the notebook from his backpack and —

"YOU THREE!" shouted a voice.

Ms. Vanderpants came storming across the playground.

"Explain yourselves!" she said.

"Uh, we didn't do this," Alexander said. "At least, not *all* of it!"

Ms. Vanderpants frowned. "I know you didn't do *this*," she said. "But you shouldn't be on school grounds on a Saturday. We're dealing with a major" — she glanced at the crack in the building — "pest problem."

"Um, sorry, Ms. Vanderpants," said Alexander. He turned to his friends. "We were just leaving."

They got out of there.

"Pest problem?!" said Nikki. "What was that about? And besides — she should be *thanking* us! We saved the school!"

"Totally!" said Rip. "The S.S.M.P. bashed the mighty P-rex and licked the candy-saurus!"

"Yeah!" said Alexander. "It was pretty sweet!" He grabbed his pencil and made a new entry.

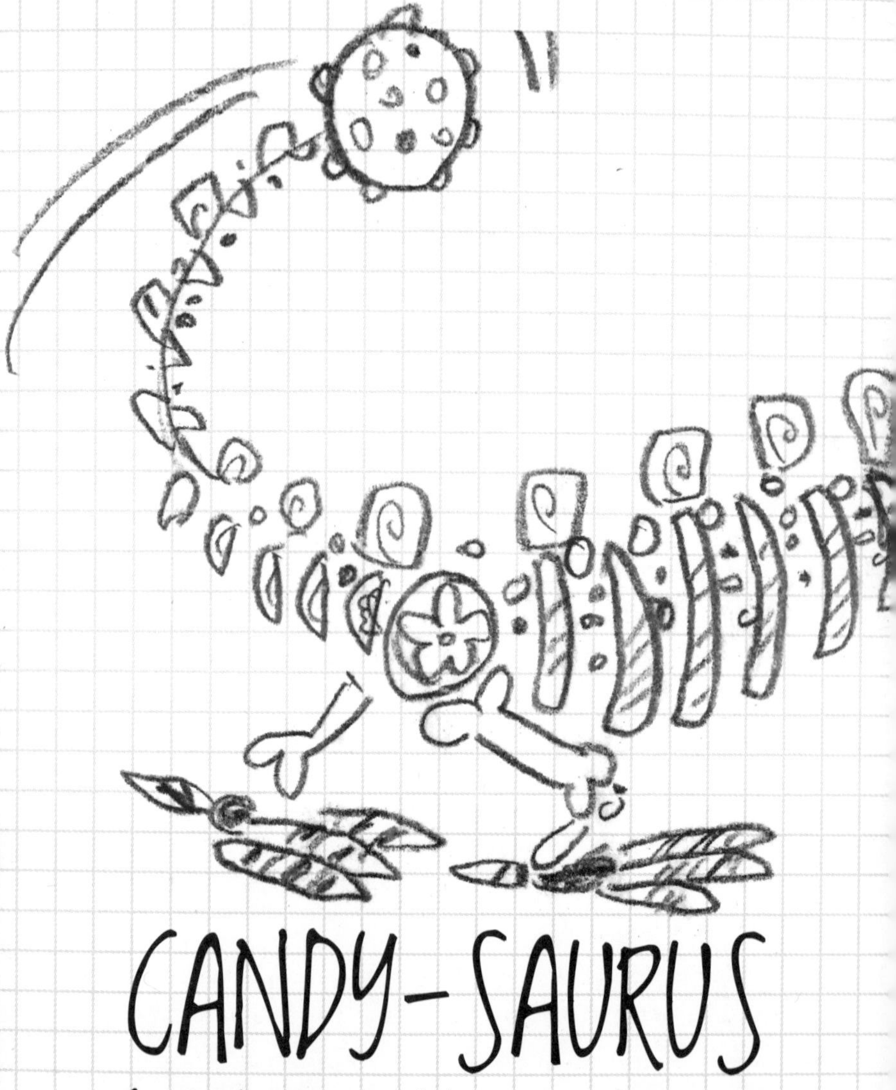

CANDY-SAURUS

A giant dino-skeleton made of candy.

HABITAT Inside a P-rex!